D0464081

A DELIGHT...

WINTER WONDERS

This Series includes the following titles:

WINTER WONDERS
SUMMER DAYS
AUTUMN FRIENDS
SUPER SPRINGTIME

SNOW TIME

All through the long winter night, snow had fallen heavily. When Ossie Otter woke up in the morning, it seemed that the whole world had turned white. He had spent the night cuddled close to his mother in their home on the river bank, and he was warm and happy. As he gazed out at the newly-white world, he knew this was a time for fun, too.

Otters love to play, and he had learnt that very special sorts of games can be played in the snow. He was off as soon as he had eaten, and his mother did not try to stop him.

THE SWAN

Ossie hoped to find a furry, four-legged friend to play with, but the first creature he saw as he padded along the river bank was a swan.

How beautiful it looked to Ossie! If he had not seen it before, and recognised its bright yellow beak and dark face, he might have thought it was made of the snow around him.

It turned a kindly eye to him, and he did think of asking it to play, but it was very big. He just gave a bark of greeting and goodbye, and hurried along, following the river.

THE KINGFISHER

Higher up the river, another bird sat on a branch, looking down into the water. Leaping in and out of the little snowdrifts in his path, Ossie came up to the bird, a kingfisher.

The kingfisher was too busy to play. He was looking into the river for his breakfast. When he saw it, he would go diving straight into the water with his wings folded over his back, to come up and out almost at once with a tasty fish.

Fish were few and far between today. He would eat if he was patient, and Ossie left him to his waiting.

THE DUCK

The next bird Ossie saw had eaten too much. As you may know, he was a duck, a mallard, and Ossie and he were friends.

Otters swim well, and the duck would often fly low over Ossie when he was in the river, making him dive under water. Sometimes, too, they would play who could dive the fastest. If Ossie won, he would get his tail nipped!

Today, the children from the nearby houses had come early with their mummies to feed the ducks, and they had made sure the mallard would not be hungry.

THE SNOWMAN

These are the children who had fed the ducks. Now they are building a snowman. From left to right they are Diana, Lucy, and Lucy's brother, Tim. Point to them as you say their names.

The snowman is in the garden of Diana's home. Do you think he looks jolly? He is wearing a straw hat called a boater, which belongs to Diana's great-granddad, and her mummy's red scarf.

Diana's mummy also gave Lucy a red balloon from their Christmas decorations, for the snowman to hold. The children called him Sam.

THE ROBIN

Ossie heard the merry laughter of the children as he scrambled through the snow. He was beginning to guess that most other young animals were sleeping through the cold weather, and he was wondering how he could have fun by himself.

Then the children's laughter died away, as they went in to lunch. In its place, he heard a cheerful whistling, calling to him.

It was this little bird, a robin, sitting on Diana's garden fence. Ossie understood his call, and followed him into the garden.

OSSIE MEETS SAM

There was Sam the snowman, in his boater, red scarf, and holding his red balloon. The robin perched on Sam's hat, still whistling, and Ossie stood and stared.

The robin was telling him he knew Ossie wanted to have fun, but he was too small to play with him. Would this big fellow be a play-mate, instead? Ossie saw this big fellow was truly built of snow, and could not play, either — but the balloon would make a lovely toy. He did not think the kind children would mind him borrowing it.

BOUNCY BALLOON

Away went Ossie with the balloon floating from his paw. As he scampered through the snow, it bumped and bounced behind him, then banged him on the head and bobbed off.

That was when Ossie found out he could make the balloon move along just by tapping it with his head — heading it, as footballers do.

Goldie, Diana's pony, thought Ossie was very clever, and Ossie thought so, too. He bounded up and down, heading the balloon across Goldie's field, until he found another exciting toy.

A SLIDEY RIDE

Can you see what Ossie's second toy is? It is a tray. Diana had dropped it from her toy box, after having a dollies' picnic in Goldie's field.

A tray is not usually very exciting, but it is when you have it as a sledge. As soon as Ossie saw the tray, he knew how to use it.

WHEEEEE! down the nearby slope he sped, the balloon flying along with him. The robin, perched on some holly bushes along the way, gave a little trilling whistle that seemed to be a laugh. For one whole hour Ossie had his slidey ride.

THE PRICKLY BUSH

Have you ever heard grown-ups say that all good things must come to an end? Sadly, that is often true. Ossie's fun came to an end suddenly, when his tray-sledge slid sideways in the snow.

Ossie landed up against the holly bushes, the red balloon touched one of the leaves, and ... BANG! Holly leaves are very prickly, and the leaf burst Ossie's balloon.

A minute later he heard Diana calling from the door of her house, not very far away, and he ran. He was afraid she might be cross.

THE OWL

The nearest place Ossie could hide was amongst the roots of a big tree, but as he quickly curled up there he heard a voice above him.

He had woken the wise old owl who lived in the tree, and the owl had a few scolding screeches to say about this noisy little nuisance.

When Ossie blinked up sadly, holding the burst balloon, he forgave the young otter. He gazed round from his high branch and gave advice. As far as Ossie understood, the owl told him to go and search — and he would find another toy.

THE LAST MEETING

Carefully Ossie left the tree. Where would he find another toy? He had found two near the houses. Perhaps there would be another near them.

Pushing through snow up to his tummy, he came across the last two feathered friends he was to meet that day. Do you know what these fine birds are called? Well, they are pheasants.

Leaning on their branch, Ossie whistled, as otters can, asking if they had seen anything he could have as a toy. They called back, softly, and looked at something higher up the branch.

THE LITTLE GIRL

As the owl had seen, someone had visited that branch before Ossie and the pheasants. Can you say who it is? You may guess because of her red and white hat, green gloves and brown coat with red cuffs. You saw her earlier, making Sam Snowman with Lucy and Tim. It is Diana. As snow begins to fall, and she hurries home, you may think she looks like a snow princess! Now Diana had seen Ossie playing, and saw him burst the balloon.

After he had run away, as she called, she brought out a present for him.

THE NEW TOY

Look at Ossie playing with his present from Diana! It is another red balloon, which he found fixed to the bush where the pheasants were perched.

This balloon he carried away carefully until he was well clear of prickly holly bushes. Then he practised his heading — and a grand new game he invented, which we can only call footing!

Ossie was going to have long, fun-filled days with his new toy. Let me let you into a secret, too — his mummy joined in the fun. It was a wonderful winter for them both.